A Yummy Snack

Patricia Brennan
Photographs by Nancy Sheehan

Rigby

Do you want to make a yummy snack?
Then do what the book says.
You need these things.

bowl  spoon

cup  tablespoon

A Yummy Snack

- 2 cups oatmeal
- 1 cup honey
- 1 cup peanut butter
- 2 cups coconut
- 1 cup raisins
- 4 tablespoons nuts

Mix. Roll into little balls.

Get two cups and
fill the cups with oatmeal.
Now put the oatmeal in the bowl.

Get one cup and
put honey in it.
Now put the honey in the bowl.

Fill two cups with coconut.

Then put peanut butter in one cup.

Now put the coconut and peanut butter in the bowl.

Now put raisins in one cup.
Then put the raisins in the bowl.

Put in 2 tablespoons of nuts.
Then put in 2 more.
That makes 4 tablespoons!

Mix with a big spoon.

Then make little balls.

Now you have a yummy snack!